A CUT IN THE SAFETY NET

FALLBLIND

FALLBLIND INDUSTRIES

Text copyright © 2023 FALLBLIND

The moral right of the author has been asserted

Published by Fallblind Industries

Cover Design Copyright © Fallblind Industries
Typeset and arranged by Up & Up Media, Australia

All rights reserved. This book is sold subject to the condition that it shall not be lent, hired out, or circulated in any form of binding or cover other than that in which it is published. No part of this work may be reproduced, stored in a retrieval system, or transmitted in any form without the prior written permission of the author, except in the case of brief quotations correctly and clearly credited to the author using handle @fallblind_

First published 2023

ISBN 978-0-6484938-8-4

Printed and bound locally: Australia, USA, UK

Do you think they'd hold a press conference;
Or try to sweep it under the rug?
Would our faces be on the cover of magazines?
I wonder what images they would use.
Surely it would be the one,
With the pistol to my head.
I cannot think of any other photo,
That would suffice.

They'll make a martyr out of me.

~Begin transmission

A CUT IN
THE
SAFETY NET

L'appel du vide...

How would I start it?

In fact,
How would I end it?
Would I apologise?
Would I try to explain,
Exactly what's going on in my head;
That led me to the conclusion,
That this,
Is the only way out?

Would I single out people,
By name?
And if so;
Who?
And what exactly,
Could I say,
That would make everything feel ok?

I'm sorry;

I'm getting ahead of myself here.

***~Titled 'untitled'*鞋**

I'm not bred,
Of cookie cutter mentality.
I don't follow the crowd;
Or aim to fit into the mould.
I'm not what you may call,
'Normal'.
I revel in the strange.
A tangible taste,
For the unusual.
An unguided misfit,
Securing his place,
Below the sun.

I don't strive to be you,
As you,
Do not strive to be me.

Let's keep it simple here.

~*This is not an act (of defiance)*

Do you truly believe,
Within your heart of hearts,
That you would have been happy,
Been content;
With the 'white picket fence'?
The days all bleeding into one?
The insurances?
The policies?
Do you truly believe,
The lack of adventure,
'1 meat and 3 veg' lifestyle,
Would have appeased your appetite?

Please!

The chaos,

Is where you shine.

~Letter to myself #432

I'm not an animal.
I'm just a product,
Of your making.
Just a,
Visual representation,
Of what the world,
Can do.

I will not project,
My past,
Onto you.

No.

You will never get close enough for that.

I am not ashamed,
Of the distance I keep.

Believe me;
I have truly,
Learnt my lesson.

~The Shield

Methods of avoidance.

I withdrew slowly,
Back into the static;
And watched it all unfold,
Through the glimmer of white noise.

I wasn't myself,
But more,
The pilot of this body for now.

Something else had taken the wheel,

And left me to shatter in the void.

~Disassociated

For I cannot live like them.
In frightened places.
Revelling in the mundane.
Content with a,
Boring job.
Boring friends.
A boring,
Missionary,
Relationship.

Instead,
I slice a cut in the safety net.
Free fall through the madness.
Laugh at the anarchy.

Land with a smile.

For I taunt the things of danger;
The beauty of chaos.

In fact,
The only thing I am afraid of,

Is being just like them.

~The stray ant

The sunlight bursts through a crack,
In the curtains.
Waking me up,
As the glow of her phone dims;

And she pretends to be asleep.

~Just add salt

I push the piston down.
My vision turns to sound.
And all these promises,
I've made to myself,
They aren't so clear.

I take these future plans,
And crush them in my hands.

All the embers fade,

And everything just,

Disappears.

~*The distraction*

3 words to suspend me.
3 words to keep me holding on,
With white knuckle grip.
Through the torture,
And the torment.
3 words to erase,
And ignite,
The pain.
3 words to float me to the sky,
Or drag me to my knees.
3 words to change the future,
Or re-evaluate the past.
3 words to heal the wound,
Or irritate the scar.

3 words.

'I love you'

~These words are weapons

Somewhere,
Out there,
A cupid has entered,
The 5th stage,
Of grief.
For a job left,
Unfinished.

Somewhere,
Out there,
Angels are consoling each other.
For such a tragic,

Failed kinship.

Somewhere,
Out there,

We lost our way.

~Fallen angels

The kindest people,
Are hurting the most.
Look far,
Beyond the facade,
They create.

The kindest people,
Are fighting demons,
You will never understand.

Yet still offer,

What little light,

They have left.

~The kindest people

I've no idea,
Where I'm running to.
Nor that,
From which I run.

But the freedom,

Truly ignites me.

~Prosthetic truths

Not love,
Not money;
Not sex,
Nor beauty.

The things I seek,

Cannot be categorised;

So fluently.

~*Seek and destroy*

And what if this is,
Just a misinterpretation?
My fragile ego,
Swaying above the flames.
My flaws transparent;

And you.

Holding the torch,

Lighting the way.

~*The torch*

Jilted lover,

Come and save me,

From this mundane,

Tranquil,

Torture.

~Seduced by the mayhem

There is nothing in this world,
That will kill you,

As softly,

As slowly,

As beautifully;

As love will.

~Slow burn

I prayed,
To raise a family with you.
To sit on a porch swing,
Elderly,
And reflect on all that has been.

But now,
I just stare;
At these empty hands.

Hands that held you.

Hands that encouraged.

Hands that soothed.

I miss you.

So fucking much.

~When the bough breaks

I hate it here.
I hate the darkness.
I hate the cold.
I hate the smell of rust,
And decay;
That lingers in every corner.
I hate the torment.
I hate the torture.
I hate the memories,
That bind it all together.
I hate the self loathing,
And the closed off thought that,

'Better days are coming'.

I hate the apologies,
That I make to myself.
But most of all,
I hate the fact that no matter where I am,

I carry it within me.

~It's scary what a smile can hide

And what of love?

I've seen wolves,
Turn to puppies;

In the batting of an eyelid.

Rock,
To rubble,

Within the violence,
Of a breath.

Do not talk to me,
About strength.

If you have been,

Too afraid,

To be vulnerable.

~Violence of a breath

I'm black and white,
Without you.

Come and,
Bring me home.

Fill me with light.

Colour me in.

~Colour me in

3 rings.
Sitting in a box.
Deep in the back of my draw.

3 fractured lifetimes.
3 broken promises.
3 failed dreams.

3 rings,
To build the walls of trauma,
To make me second guess;

Every single touch.
Every single motive.
Every single word.

3 rings,
To remind me;

To never trust again.

~3 rings

Love her.

Cherish her.

Buy her nice things.

Treat her well,

And always put her first.

Then,

Watch how beautiful she glows,

In the arms of someone else.

~*Love and abandonment*

And then one day,
We are forced;
To write them out of the script.

But the show goes on.

No matter how often,
The characters change.

Everybody gets their time,

In the spotlight,

Before they fade.

***~Spotlight*￼**

There was a time,
Where it was just you,

And I.

We took on the whole world,

Together.

And nothing,
Was as sacred;

As us.

These are the shadows,
I bathe in.

This is the memory,

That keeps me awake;

And tears me apart.

~*The memories lair*

I am going to love you,
For the rest of my life.
Whether we are together,
Or not.
Whether we still see each other,
Or you are gone completely.

You will always be,
Deep within my heart.

And there will be times,
When the wind caresses my face,
And my smile,
Illuminates the sun;

I will think of you fondly;
And forever appreciate,

The time we had.

~The promise

Good morning.

Just checking your vitals.

Roll up your sleeve.

This should alleviate the pain.

~Remedy

I don't want to feel,
Anymore.

So;

As the eyes roll back,
And the synapses disengage.

Remember me,

For who I was;

And enjoy the fucking show.

~Showtime

Because I don't believe,
In love anymore.

And that is all,

That I had left.

~*Defeated*

This Abyss,
Romances me so freely.
This void in which I lay.
Propped up by pharmaceuticals,

Yet still dead to the world.

I can feel you with me,
But the darkness remains.
Time is fluid;
As days don't interpret as they used to.

Your faces blur,
As in within a dream.
I know you are here,

But I,

Am light years away.

~*Light years away*

It's not that I wanted to die.
It's just,
I didn't want to be alive,
For that period of my life.
I didn't feel,
Like I was strong enough;
To make it through.

But here I am.
On the other side.

That's the thing about life,
And heartache.
We generally survive;

But there is a massive part of us,

That dies getting to the destination.

~*The otherside*

It's getting exhausting,
This;
Drinking myself to death.
I remember when,
I did it for fun.
I remember when it wasn't every night.
And now,
I'm just drinking,

To fill a void.

To harbour the sorrow.

To kill the pain.

Just for a little while.

~Live forever/ Die tonight

Wild and free,
Slowly formed into,

Lonely;

And trapped,

Within myself.

There is a great divide,

Between what you tell yourself;

And what is real.

~The actuality of events

Within this silence,
I watch the fragments of my life,
Circle me;
Like a tornado.
I can reach out,
And pick pieces away.
Like grains of sand.

Within this silence,
The veiled blur,

Between truth,
And lie,

Collides.

Crashing every thought to the floor.

Tonight,

The whole world falls apart,

~Within this silence

My intentions made evident,
As you wipe them from your lips.
How do you show me,
Any emotive response?

I don't even exist.

Just a fragment of your own,
Crippled imagination.

This isn't real.

The version of me,
You pray,
And wish,
That I could be;

Is a long time dead.

~Crippled imagination

These demons pull at me.
Subtracted thought,
Still divide;
Yet portray addition to my life.

Because these thoughts,
And triggers,
Don't ever disappear.

Perpetually,

I do not feel comfortable.

It's not you,

It's me.

~*It's not you, It's me*

Transitioning methods of,
manipulation.
Infused with,
Alcohol,
And cocaine.

Edging closer toward,

The brink of self destruction.

The situation intensifies.

The irises widen.

Within this chaos,

I am home.

~The brink of self destruction

There is a disruption,
Between my mind,
And my heart;
That you are,

Actually gone.

I wake up,
Every morning,
Still expecting to see you.

But you are no longer there.

And so the day turns to black,
And the dark rim circles my vision again.

~Tidal wave

Animated into existence.
Prosthetic,
Some may say.
But believable,
All the same.
The colours intensify,
As the sound grows sharp.
Lingering in this void,
My mind an entity,
Of its own creation.
Time and space suspended,
Within rhythmic heartbeats.
All fear is erased.
And absolutely everything,
Is possible.

~*Lola in the sky with diamonds*

Her apprehension disarmed me.
I came in like a titan;
But she was a sniper.

Arousing me with her,
Discontent.
Pulling me further,
Into the rabbit hole.

Even if I wanted to leave,
I was stuck still.

So I stayed.

~*Halos and horned wings*

Eggs,
And beer,
And cocaine,
For breakfast.

Dreams change.

The addictions never cease,
To dissipate.

~*They label it 'functioning'*

I can still taste,
Your nectar,
Upon my lips.
I close my eyes,
And search the darkest,
Corners of my mind.

And there,
You wait.

Deep sighs,
And tense legs.

Hands bound,
And bite marks upon your skin.

This is the legacy,

You have left behind.

~The gift is a curse

'What are you doing?'

'Just writing'.

Just trying to keep,
The bottle from my hand.

The drugs,
From these veins.

The gun,
From this mouth.

'What am I doing?'

~Just writing

They will never understand,
These issues.
Hell,
I can't even understand them.
The triggers.
The constant hunger.
The inability to stay close,
But still needing to feel 'validated'.
The fear.
The reclusiveness.

The sadness behind the smile.

'It's hard not to like you fuck boy.'

She whispered.

'Give it a few days...'

~*The carousel*

I will never forgive.
I will never forget.
I will use this illusion,
As a proxy;
To harden the shell,
And deaden the eyes.

I will let the cancer,
Of love;
Consume me.

Until I am pale.

Until I am weak.

I will never forgive.
I will never forget.

~Never forgive/Never forget

I pull at the stitch,
And watch the seams unravel.
Without hesitation,
I slip right through the fold;

A cut in the safety net.

The opposing side of the mirror.

Leaving my former self,
To sit abandoned.

Barring a clean slate.

An empty canvas;

To rebuild a monster.

~A cut in the safety net

I'm not afraid of death.
In fact,
Quite the opposite.

I've been praying for it.

~*Gospel*

Rape my body,
Again.
I'd far prefer,
You destroy my flesh,
Than continue the damage,
You're doing to my head.

Force me down,
And slut me out.
But keep my sanity,
Intact.

I'm running out of,
'Happy places',
To go to;

When your body,

Is pressed to mine.

~*Happy Places*ND

If making me the villain,
Of your story,
Helps you;
With moving on,
And letting go.

Then,

Slay. Queen. Slay.

~*Slay/Queen/Slay*

And I feel the thorns stab deep inside.
Gripping me.
Pulling me back in.
Telling me that there is somewhere I would rather be.
That love is not 2 bodies holding each other,
But more,
One body combusting inside.

Pierce my veins.
Fire my lungs.

Home is not what I thought it would be.

~There's no place called home

At first it was a bee sting.
An itch I could not stop scratching.
A gnawing at my chest I just couldn't shake off.

And it grew.

God,
Did it grow.

And as much as I tried,
To push it away,

The bigger it just seemed to get.

The urgency of the matter somewhat aroused me.

As I played with her hair;

And flirted with the trigger.

~Trigger

And then it becomes,
A game of numbers.
A collection of hearts.
An inferno of,

Prosthetic emotions;

And broken promises.

~Heaven changes

The ghost of you,
Still lingers upon my lips.
It still draws me in,
And holds me close.
It still keeps me cold,
Throughout the night.

And pulls on every single thread,

That is left of my sanity.

~The ghost of you

The world is not a rom com.
It's not Tinseltown starlets;
And Braun men.

Overcoming obstacles;
To get back together.

It's not impenetrable hearts,
Or montages,
With cheesy love songs.

It's a fucking horror movie.

An icicle through the chest.

And a bullet,

To the head.

The world isn't an oyster,
With a pearl inside.

No.

It's an ocean of loneliness,

In a room full of 'friends'.

~Tinseltown starlets

Happiness is,
The final frontier.
The destination;
The goal.
But do not neglect the journey.
For it is here,
That all the pieces,
Come together.

~Happiness

You're losing focus.
Too busy,
Chasing girls,
And gathering hearts.

Is this where the hurt leads you?
An inability to grasp the simple concept,
Of something potential?

Too guarded to let them in,

You are rotting to the core.

~Wake up

I fill you up with,

Money.

Sex;

And drugs.

Hoping to find the formula;

The perfect measurements;

To take away the pain.

~The cauldron

I hide in the darkness.
Shadowing your every thought.

What you see,
I see.
What you hear,
I hear.
What you know,
I know.

I have been waiting here silently,
For your entire life.

Feeding.
Growing.

I can control how you think.
I can control how you feel.

I might not be the one to hold the gun,

But I'll make damn sure you pull the trigger.

~Internal narrative

I pushed myself,
To shaking point.

Completely fractured,
Every ounce of my being.

So I could pick up,
All of the pieces;

And start again.

~Resurrection

Something is happening.

It's picking at the skin,

And festering in the eyes.

What becomes of this,
I have no idea.
But there is a shift.

A movement.

A distorted sound,

That I cannot place my finger on;

But I know it's abundant.

Something magnificent,

Is about to endure.

~The outer layers of static

I could run away,
From all of this.
I could start again,
Somewhere new.
Find new experiences.
Make new friends.
Manifest new dreams.

I could completely rebuild,
My life.

Or,

I could stay right here.

And burn this motherfucking place to the ground.

~Life choices

I dawned in this eclipse.
I blindly shadowed the moon,
And made the stars my own.
All of your power is gone.
For I am the sun.
I am the earth.
I am the air you breathe,
And the ground you walk.
I am your sinner;
Your saint.
Your devil;
Your god.

I am alive,

Within you.

~Meta

You are not,

The missing piece.

You're the whole fucking puzzle.

~Jigsaw*gsaw

I have made,
Billions of decisions,
That I haven't been,
Entirely sure about.

But you.

I was always sure about you.

~No hesitation

We made plans,

To catch up often.

But I knew,

From the moment you left;

That I was never going to see you again.

~One last glance (before I go)

I still dream of you,
In the witching hour.

I will never confess this;

But you still invade my thoughts,
And erode my mind.

I still wake up,
Wishing you were here.
Knowing,
That you never will be;

Again.

~The witching hour

Maybe I just need to reset.
Tuck myself away,
Just for a little while.
Maybe I don't want to be strong,
Anymore.
Maybe I want to shatter,
And lay in pieces,
On the bathroom floor.
Maybe I'm tired.
Maybe I'm emotionally exhausted.

Maybe,

I'm just fucking over it.

~Ctrl/Alt/Del

You made me feel,

So useless.

So damn,
Unpretty.

And there was nothing,

That I could do about it.

~Unpretty

I'm just,
Aloft.

An alcoholic;

A drug addict;

A waste.

I'm conventional,
To society's standards.

But I'm also lying,

To everyone I know.

~Conventional

A simple life,
Is what I crave.
But with these walls,
I'm still a slave.
I sabotage,
And set alight.
The very things,
I want from life.

~A simple life

The healing never truly begins.
Because I always remember,
The things I am trying to forget.

I drench it in ether,
And coat it with cocaine;
But still it sits in wait.

For the comedown to arise.

I will never truly be free,
Until my dying breath.

Some things cannot be forgotten.
Some things cannot be erased.

The healing,

Never truly,

Begins.

~*The healing never truly begins*

And sometimes,
You just don't exist anymore.

Not to your friends,
Or your family,
Or the guy who gives you your cigarettes at the corner store.

You just don't exist anymore.

And that's ok.

~Invisibility (is my superpower)

I knew we were falling apart.
But that's the thing about hope.
It's relentless.
It will keep you awake at night.

Gnawing at your mind,
Until all that is left;

Is the cold shivering hands,

Of a tired,

Broken,

Lonely,

Man.

~*Cold shivering hands*

Things are just,

'Things'.

A collective.
Possessions.
Decor.

A collection of false happiness.
A collection of ways I have,
Tried to trick myself.

As I look around at these objects;
I guess,
They're just a placebo;

For the loneliness.

But the heart knows different.

The heart knows,
This is a lie I've told myself,
Time and time again.

~The heart knows

Nothing here,
Makes sense.
But maybe,
It's not supposed to.

Maybe,
Within this void,

I am learning,

To love myself.

~Inner child

I'll always be looking for you.
Within the eyes of strangers.
In the warmth of hugs.
Between words of songs;
And scenes of movies.

I will always search for the pieces,

That remind me of you.

~*Within the eyes of strangers*

I overloved,
As per usual.

I bled away,
Rational thought.

And just let the feelings,
Consume me.

I need to take ownership,

For the part,
That I played.

~Self assessment

I miss you.

I miss your laugh.
I miss your presence.
I miss the way your eyes,
Light up when you smile.

I miss the way you make me feel.
I miss your arms,
Wrapped around me.

But most of all,

I miss the way,

You used to miss me too.

~Growing up/Growing apart

The insanity keeps me illuminated.
Maybe,
Knowing my next move,
Works for you.
But for me,
It is harrowing.

I don't want you to know,
What happens next.

My capabilities,

Are fucking endless.

~The machine will stop when it is satisfied

I guess,
The thing I miss about her most,
Is her eyes.

And her lips.

The way she made me feel,
So complete.

No matter how incomplete,
It turns out I am.

The thing I miss about her most,

Is the way,

She felt like home.

~Home has a heartbeat

You knew,
Exactly,
How to destroy me.

And you did it,
So effortlessly.

So beautifully.

~*Effortless*

I isolated myself.
I tucked myself away,
Like I did,
When I was a child.
I completely disappeared,
Without knowing,
If I was ever coming back.

But it was in this silence,
This darkness,
That I reinvented.
And came back,
With hardened wings.

***~Reinvention*brace

Dear Lola.

Nothing is getting better,
But I guess,
Nothing is getting worse.
I love you now,
As I loved you then.

But those 3 words haven't done either of us any favours,

In a long while.

~*(Sadly) all tomorrows become yesterdays*

It still hurts.
It never stopped.
You just don't know about it.
You didn't have to deal with it,
At 1:37am.

When I was paralysed by you.

I've become so well,
At hiding it;
You wouldn't even know it was there.

But I do.

Because I feel it.

Every minute;
Of every,

Single,

Day.

It still hurts.

***~Paralysis*brace

I am far more frightened,
Of how much longer,
This will persist.
Than what I am,
Of ending it all,
Entirely.

~Time bomb

There are,
In a sense;
Tokens of me left behind.

Songs on the radio.
Places,
We have been.
Memories;
That cast you into reflection,
Of a life you have endured.

Scars.

Secrets.

Promises.

Somewhere beneath the undertow,
Of glimmering light;
You will eventually scratch the surface,

And find me there.

~Beneath the surface

This is not the end.
It only just began.
I'll pick you up,
So I can tear you down again.
And there is nothing real.
Just illusions you can't kill.

The flame.
The pain.
The shame.
The blame.

And all that's left.

This endless fucking need;

To bring you to your knees.

~Self Vs Self

And sometimes,
People use their power,
To hurt,
And neglect.
And the saddest,
Most brutal,
Thing is;

We will let them.

Over and over again.

Because;

We live in hope that things will change.

We live in hope that they will remember.

Because,

Love.

~*Because/Love*

I don't own you.

I don't own,
Anything.

Gifts that arise,
Are just,
For now.

I want you to be happy.

I want you to fulfil,

All of your dreams.

You deserve the universe.

I'm just glad,
I could for a moment,

Be a part of yours.

~*Gifts that arise*

Love,
As a concept;

Destroyed me.

It took everything,
That meant the most;

And just,

made it disappear.

Love,
As a concept,
Was temporary.

But the pain,

Within reflection;

Will linger forever.

**~*Love as a concept*

Let them eat cake.

Let them choke on the fumes,
Of their own,
Security.

Let them,

Lie to themselves,

About the illusions;
In which they bathe.

Let them destroy each other.

Let them eat cake.

~*Let them eat cake*

I live,

As I love.

Unapologetic.

Fierce.

And with ample amounts,

Of absolute insanity.

~Unapologetic

This is my everlasting statement.
Trace your fingers across the words,
Until the ink bleeds through your skin.
Feel the upheaval,
Of all your desires;
Hum and glow inside.
Like trapped fireflies,
On a warm summer's night.

Let the vibrance guide you,
To places you would much rather be.
Stare deep into the abyss,
And from it;
Cast your dreams into fruition.

For each day is unlike the last.
Yet a reckoning,
Unto how much you care to gain,
Opposed;
How much there is to lose.

Make this day,
Yours.

~Fireflies

Love,

With everything that you have.

With every fibre,
Of your being.

There is not enough time,

In this life;

To love in halves.

Give all that you can;

Give all that you've got.

Love,

With everything you have.

~*Not enough time*～

It will not happen suddenly,
But somewhere within longevity.
The minutes turn to hours.
The hours to days.
The days to weeks and before long;

You will not think of me at all.

Calculating distance as time.

The further between ticks of the clock,
The more the memory of me shall surpass.

This is the true form of disappearance.

The delicate art,

Of fading away.

~The delicate art of fading away

There are lessons,
I have learnt.
Not necessarily taught to me,
But learnt,
All the same.
There are lessons,
I have survived.
Lessons,
I have endured.
Behind closed doors.
Behind closed eyes.
And deep within,
The most intimate of moments.

The creation,
Of something so disastrous.

So,

Damaging;

Once began,
As something,

Beautiful.

~Beautiful

Occasionally,

You will think of me.
And my only hope is,
Your memories are as sweet,
As mine.
I hope the chaos,
Eludes you.
And the sun upon my face,
And the glint in my eye,
Is all that you can see.

One day,
I hope the feeling,
My memory gives you;
Is the same,
As you gave me.

~Porcelain

One day,
I am going to walk out this door;
And never walk back through it again.
In this time,
Please don't be sad.
Just register that this is unfortunately,
A part of life.
Always remember,
I loved you more than you could ever begin to imagine.
Since the time each of you were born,
I have done everything within my power,
To make you happy.
To keep you safe.
And to hopefully make you proud.
As I am of you.
Wash away the times I was sad,
And just remember my smile.

That smile,

Was because of you.

I love you eternally.

Always.

Dad.

~A letter to my children

Because it is only,
Within my dreams,
That I still see you.

And if I must sleep,
To be with you again;

Then I will sleep,

Forevermore.

~Forevermore

And I collect up,
All of my belongings,
And make it all;

Disappear.

Like I didn't even exist.

This place is so empty now.

And I'm still talking to myself.

~Matthew 27:5

They may not understand my decisions;
But they weren't there when I decided them.
They weren't there for the neglect.
They weren't there for the abuse.
They weren't there for the torment,
Or the torture,
Or the pain.

And they certainly weren't there,

When I needed them most.

~*Decisions*

Backing away slowly,
So it won't hurt as much,
When I am gone.
Erasing all importance,
That I may have had.
And watching the world,
Move on without me.

The sun still shines,
And the birds still sing.

When I finally depart,

Hopefully;

You won't feel a thing.

~My gift to you

Who will be,
The first to find out?
Will my employer,
Call my family?
Or my family,
My employer?
So many questions,
I wish I was around,
To know the answers to.

~Between staggered breaths

I can see the finish line.
The end,
To this beautiful tragedy.
And as a tear formulates,
In my eye.
I wonder how,
It could have been.
If everything was just,
Different.
How would have things,
Turned out then?

~A different path

Black out the days.
Black out the sun.

Tear down the shades,

Shut down the machine,

And delete.

Remove yourself,
And go back to zero.

Don't explain yourself.
Don't present your case.

Just disappear.

Black out the days.
Black out the sun.

~*Black out the sun*

Special Thanks

I'd like to quickly take this opportunity to whole heartedly thank the following people for their undying support. Whether it be with my writing, my lifestyle, or my 'at times' unhinged perspective of the world around me.

Teneille White
Stephanie Katastrophy
Deanna Black
Yolanda Sloan
Kylie Blacker
Danielle Cameron (Marino)
Lauren Christiansen
Dean McKenzie
Peta Page
Nikki Harris
Pete Walstab
Candice Harwood
Ander Louis
Renee Reed
Jodie Douglas
Amanda Stirton
Aaron Moore
Matt McKenzie
Max Murray
Beau Cherry
Jamie Schultz
Darcy Mim
Peter (Pedro) Marshall
The Sarahs
The Jessicas
The Katies

And most notably;

Lola.

@fallblind_

www.ingramcontent.com/pod-product-compliance
Lightning Source LLC
Chambersburg PA
CBHW040742020526
44107CB00084B/2846